WALKING TRACKS AND BUSHF
ON SYDNEY ADVENTIST HOSPI
(AND ADJACENT RESERVE
IN THE WAHROONGA – NORMANI
(On which they are kind enough to allow responsi

BLUE GUM

MOUNT PLEASANT A

PINE ST. FIRE TRAIL

MYRTLE STREET

COMENARRA TRACK

THE COMENARRA PARKWAY

KEY

Fire Trails (2 metres (+) wide)	
Well – made paths and tracks	
Well – defined tracks	
Steep and / or rough tracks	
Poorly-defined / steep / rough tracks	
Reserves - Woodland	
Reserves - Grass or open land	
Rivers, Creeks or Pondage	

N

Heights
in Metres

SCALE

0   100   200   300 metres

For details of tracks and trails South of this area, see "Walking Trails of the Lane Cove Valley",
scale 1 : 10,000 , available at Map Shops or via STEP inc PO Box 697, Turramurra, NSW, 2074

SEE INSET BELOW

INSET
SEE TOP RIGHT

Frankie is an ecologist and writer who has worked and volunteered in entirely too many different roles, including as a legal research assistant, civil servant, freelance journalist, and snake relocator.

Frankie writes and ecologises from a small house and garden shared with a cat named Evie and a flock of bossy chickens.

WATERWAY

An adult Powerful Owl carefully preens its feathered legs.

WATERWAY

Frankie O'Brien
on behalf of

Lulu.com
2024

O'Brien, Frankie

Waterway

First published in 2018.

Revised edition published in 2025.

ISBN 978-0-244-13152-4

Guidebook – Local History – Wahroonga – Lane Cove River Catchment Environmental Science – Ecology – Environmental Management

http://www.facebook.com/wahroongawaterwayslandcare

For more writing, visit http://wildpathways.wordpress.com

Cover design by Rosemary Gosper [http://rosemarygosper.com].

Contents

Acknowledgements

I acknowledge the Indigenous people, traditional owners of the lands on which I have lived, on which I have written, on which I have worked. I acknowledge their elders, past, present, future, and rising. Indigenous sovereignty was never ceded.

Thanks go to the following people for their help in reviewing and editing this book: Chris, Hasmukh, Jill, Paul, and Terence.

Thank you to all the Wahroonga Waterways Landcare volunteers, past, present, and future. Your dedication and love of nature is inspiring. We need more of it in the world.

Thank you to those organisations that supported the Landcare group's work, and to those individuals who helped us make things happen.

Thank you also to the bush regeneration team, in all its incarnations, at Adventist Aged Care Wahroonga. Boen, Consuelo, Elissa, Iman, John, Lester, Milan, Raphael, Ryan, Violy, and Zhao, you were a blast to work with, and I learnt a lot from you. Thanks to Jayden who enthusiastically took on the role I left behind.

Thanks to Graham for teaching me the ropes. You gave me my first real start after a few false ones.

And finally, thank you, to you who have picked up this book. You are most important of all. We need your support to continue protecting this bushland, and all nature.

Foreword

by Graham Wegener

The background to this book starts on the 1 July 2003 when I took on the role of landscaper for the Waratah Way development of 20 villas and 30 apartments at Adventist Aged Care Wahroonga. This started with the assistance of one groundsman, and when we were not doing grounds work, we did bush care. Half of the first day was spent pulling Privet.

As the build progressed, with a bobcat and tipper purchased, the team increased to 12 during college breaks. These lads showed me what they had been up to the previous year under the tutelage of the aged care manager Bob Butler, a self taught bush regenerator. What I encountered were two models of the Pyramids of Giza. Piles of Privet where the machete wielding lads had competed to throw their victim weed to the apex of the four metre pile. There were Privet stumps everywhere along the banks below Kents Gully but east of that you entered a veritable forest of Broad- and Small-leafed Privet, with intermittent house sized walls of Balloon Vine and Lantana.

As 2005 saw the aged care grounds revamped, landscaping and a renovation project draw to a close, the manager walked me, or should I say part-crawled along the one track that wound its way to the eastern end of the Wahroonga Estate. Crawling through one Lantana tunnel I thought I was never going to see the light of day again, it was the height of a three storey building. He proposed that I stay on with the team of lads and restore the bush as we had done for the Waratah Way development. I said, "You have to be joking" and I had only seen 300m of the four kilometre creek line. At least, I thought there was a creek somewhere, under all that Privet, Lantana, Balloon Vine and Blackberry.

'Another landscape project' was the attitude I took on the bush but this was to change in 2011 when we tendered for the work of a 192-page Biodiversity Management Plan of the now gazetted

E2 Environmental Conservation Zone, Wahroonga Estate. Attending the National Landcare Conference in 2012 got me motivated, seeing hundreds of other people as mad as I, but it was a struggle during the first two years; still establishing maintenance trails, 100-page reports to the Federal Department of Environment and trying to set up a monitoring program.

Then in May 2014 along came environmental scientist Frances. Things changed over the next four reports with establishment of a dedicated bush nursery to produce plants of local provenance and an external audit that had us on the hop with stepping up our required monitoring program.

Frances' professionalism had established Wahroonga Waterways Landcare as a community entity with grants from Ku-ring-gai Council, Department of Environment, and Land Services NSW to advance the restoration. With a grant from Grill'd, we even bought dedicated shirts with a Variegated Fairy-wren emblem that Frances designed. (Thank you to our resident volunteer naturalist Jillian Nolan for capturing the alluring photo in the valley that became the basis for the design).

With the establishment of a dedicated volunteer day each Tuesday morning 8:45 to 12:30 came regular volunteers (all welcome, it's a great pot luck morning tea at 10). It can't be overstated how great an inspiration it is to have volunteers work with you. Because of the long term nature of regeneration work you sometimes feel you are fighting a losing battle and along come volunteers that motivate you. You can't help but focus, sharing with them the successes. I, like Frances, would like to name them all one by one, but best not start less you miss one as they have all been precious to the restoration.

Another inspiration is the visiting environmental school classes and Planet Ark School Tree Day plantings. Thank you dedicated teachers, community volunteers and schools; you actually drive our yearly restoration planning.

With Frances came a dedicated environmental scientist working as one with the biosphere of Coups Creek. I have been privileged to work with both and together you have changed me into an environmentalist. Thank you both, you have helped develop me four-fold:

1. Physically – Yes, a 31.4 ha site with up to 70m ascent keeps you fit.
2. Mentally – You need to be constantly alert especially with a department motto for Grounds and Bush teams of "Don't let a weed go to seed" and a weed list (thank you, Frances) of 160 weeds.
3. Spiritually – As a Christian scientist I have been reaffirmed of the hand of a master designer at work. A jealous God so proud of the intricacy of what he has made that he set aside the seventh day of the week to celebrate it with Humanity.
4. Emotionally – Falling in tune with nature and helping it succeed is very soothing as it moves at its pace.

So Frances; I'm sure I'm not the only person you have touched with your care for the natural world around us.

THANK YOU for this book as it takes us on a soothing meander of Coups Creek and what is entailed in its care. It's a better waterway for your being there.

THANK YOU for the resources of $38,000 in grants and the help of volunteers that you mustered to achieve the grants and continue the restoration.

And THANK YOU for the collaborative contacts you have forged with the community and Government to help make Coups Creek and environs the gem of the Lane Cove.

Wishing you the best as you continue in your environmental career, mentoring all you come in contact with to continue the care.

Kindest regards
Graham Wegener
Grounds and Projects Supervisor
Adventist Aged Care Wahroonga
2018

Introduction

For more than three and a half years, I worked in the bushland surrounding Coups Creek as a land conservation manager. It was a workplace like no other, and one where I learnt many valuable lessons, which continue to serve me well as I carry them with me beyond the fringes of the Wahroonga bushland.

The bushland site I worked at needs to be considered from several angles. It is a habitat corridor containing two Critically Endangered Ecological Communities, a threatened species, several waterways forming the headwaters of the Lane Cove River, and walking trails open to the public. Suburban sprawl presses in on all sides, although you would not think it as you walk between the trees. Many animals have made this place their refuge. I still do not know all the species of flora and fauna that make it their home. It was greener and lusher than the ecosystems I had grown up with in Western Sydney.

Before I chose the path of environmental science, I wanted to be, at various times in my life, a veterinarian, a marine biologist, an environmental journalist, a zookeeper, and an environmental lawyer. The natural world has always fascinated me, but as a child, I had a very narrow idea of what that actually meant. I loved animals, but could not see the intricate links between them and the ecological systems that support them.

At the end of 2007, the teachers at my high school had organised for my grade to have an excursion to the local cinema. Chattering happily, we all set off walking through the suburbs for a nice day away from school to watch a newly released documentary. Its title was *An Inconvenient Truth*.

We came back shaken. Within a few weeks of watching the documentary, three of us decided to establish an environmental club, and by the start of the next school year, we had a 'green group' up and running that is still operational as I write. In that first year, we established a recycling scheme that simultaneously prevented recyclable material from ending up in a tip, and also provided an activity for the Special Education class who would gather the recycle bins from each classroom daily with great pride and ceremony.

By the time university applications rolled around, there was no doubt in my mind that I was going to study environmental science. But when, five and a half years later (my studies extended by a combined law degree), I found myself standing on the edge of over thirty hectares of urban bushland, about to start my career in land conservation management, I had no idea of the adventures ahead.

The stories contained within these pages cover a wide range of topics. There are anecdotes about animals and about article-writing, and about some of the weirder things I've seen in the bush. Tales of friends and happenings. Happy stories, sad stories, stories about setbacks and stories of hope, all set to the background of Wahroonga's bushland – its trees, its creeks and its sandstone escarpments. Stories of how we interact with them, hurt them, love them, protect them.

To some, nature has become something foreign to humanity, something separate and strange. But like it or not, we are intrinsically bound to the breathing of the seas and the alchemy of storms. Nature can survive without us, but we cannot survive without nature.

Land

Morning sunlight through the trees of Sydney Sandstone Gully Forest

LAND

Earth

I arrived to work at Wahroonga Estate in 2014. It seemed huge at first, a sixty-six-hectare property owned by the Seventh-day Adventist Church, containing the San Hospital, several schools, residences, administrative buildings, an aged care facility, and around thirty-one hectares of conservation bushland. The land to which the bush is confined is essentially a small valley that follows Coups Creek until it runs into the Lane Cove River, or *Turrumburra*, as it is known in one of the local Indigenous languages.

Development has claimed much of the Ashfield Shale geological layer. Found on the ridgetops and formed of clay-rich, dark grey Glenorie soil, Ashfield Shale was mostly removed with the construction of the San Hospital and Fox Valley Road. The last remaining strip of Ashfield Shale runs to the east and parallel to Fox Valley Road. Most of the site is dominated by the Hawkesbury Sandstone formation, the stone emerging as huge boulders and low cliffs with a thin layer of Gymea soil, an unsurprisingly sandy and low fertility type.

The valley was made an 'E2 – Environmental Conservation' zone in 2008 as a condition for redevelopment of the built areas in Wahroonga Estate. Unless rezoned, this land is not to be developed, cleared, logged or allow any activities that are not for the conservation of the environment. Part of its importance lies in the habitat corridor it provides into Lane Cove National Park, the other part being the threatened species and ecosystems it supports.

Although privately owned, the bushland is crisscrossed with walking trails utilised by the general public – bushwalkers, dog-walkers, cyclists, students, visitors to the hospital or the aged care facility, and visitors to the bush itself. For over three and a half years I walked these trails, first as the Environmental Officer managing the bushland, and then also as the Coordinator of the local Landcare Group, Wahroonga Waterways Landcare, until they became so familiar, I could follow them in the dark.

LAND

Each trail has its own character. Exposed white clay by the Bush Chapel. Rocky sands along the concrete pathway. Deep soils amongst the Sydney Turpentine Ironbark Forest. Reddish clay in the Blue Gum High Forest. Earthen rainbows run below the loam, occasionally exposed by rain or landslip. In some places, disturbed by breezes, pale dust mixes with the air, rarely rising more than half a metre from the ground. It settles on the leaves of low growing plants until the next breeze stirs them.

Air

Due to its valley structure, the bushland around Coups Creek tends to have a cooler temperature than in the urban areas surrounding it. This is also partially due to the 'urban heat island effect'; urban areas, due to the density of people, energy usage and building material present, produce and emit significant heat. A study by Dr Libby Gallagher that informed the Cool Streets initiative has shown that retention of trees and green spaces, or revegetation efforts such as rooftop gardens will reduce the heat island effect (and lower energy bills!). Studies such as that in 2007 by John Crompton of Texas A & M University demonstrate that trees improve property values, yet the first activity many people engage in when they move to a leafy suburb is to cut down the nearest tree.

The valley shape and density of trees makes the creekline a refreshing place in the summer but freezing cold in the winter. The temperature difference as you descend towards the creek is palpable – there is a clear distinction between the overlaying warm air and the sudden shock of underlying cold air halfway down a slope.

The valley's shape means that the bush within is well sheltered. Winds rarely shake the plants, although light breezes occasionally waft through. When they do, they bring with them the delicate thistledown seeds of plants like the Common Silkpod (*Parsonsia straminea*). The first time I saw these glowing white, feathery parachutes, I thought they had come from a common dandelion (*Taraxacum officinale*), and since this is a weed, I quickly went to retrieve them. I realised my mistake when I had two large handfuls – the abnormal abundance made me stop – and my eye was drawn up to the canopy, from where I observed the seeds serenely drifting down.

I could almost feel the trees breathing, standing there beneath the canopy. Out on the nearby roads, particularly the major transport artery that is Pennant Hills Road, the air is staler and often laden with pollution. Beneath the trees, the air is fresh and clean; there is something healing about taking in big lungfuls of it.

Only in fire season is this inadvisable. The air then is dry and heavy, scratching the throat and making the eyes sting. Luckily, these times are rare in the valley, and mostly within our control.

Fire

Fire has not played a large role in the valley's history, at least in modern times. Aside from the occasional hazard reduction burn, few fires have occurred, the most memorable being a fire which raced out of control in 2002 or 2003, surging upslope from Coups Creek towards the retirement village on Mount Pleasant Avenue.

Hazard reduction burns are a big operation. People living downwind of the site to be burnt must be warned a week in advance. Two fire trucks full of fire fighters would trundle along newly-cleared fire trails to the burn site, which had already been separated from the rest of the bushland by handlines – hand-cleared fire breaks. A burn is always started at the top of a slope, as fire will race up hills, quickly roaring out of control. Fire fighters along the handline monitor where the fire is, and how fast it is moving.

There were two hazard reduction burns during the years I worked in the valley. Due to the density of bushland in the catchment, only a few widely spaced areas can be burnt each year, for the safety of both wildlife and humans.

After the burn, the site is monitored for the remainder of the day and any embers extinguished. We would visit the blackened sites for weeks, looking for any sign of regrowth. Then the first bright green shoots would appear stark against the charcoal. Woody plants would coppice, Eucalypts and *Persoonia* growing back from a lignotuber under the earth, even as the air is still heavy with the smell of burning. The strappy *Xanthorrhoea* leaves start to grow back like the first fuzz of hair after a shave. The ground covers return, slowly at first, then rapidly covering the blackened earth. By spring, little evidence of a burn remains, although the trees are still a little black, the vegetation is a little dense, and there is a profusion of coppiced plants.

And then we move, a kilometre across the valley, and prepare the next site for that year's burn.

One place that will never be deliberately burnt is by the creek. The riparian corridor is considered too fragile for a burn, and the impacts on the bushland as a whole could be significant. After all, it runs through the very middle of the valley like a lifeline.

Water

Coups Creek is the highest of all the Lane Cove River's tributaries. Gathering stormwater from Lucinda Avenue, Fox Valley Road, Mount Pleasant Ave and The Comenarra Parkway, it cuts a permanent pathway in a south-westerly direction until it meets the Lane Cove River, *Turrumburra*, on the other side of The Comenarra Parkway, within the Lane Cove National Park.

The creek has many moods – dry and sluggish without rain, fiercely eager after a storm, gently contemplative during the in-between times. There is peace in sitting by the running waters, letting the flow mesmerise you, trying to follow each new bubble from sudden creation to sudden cessation, watching the twirl of tiny eddies around submerged stones. On hot days, this kind of meditation by the creek, in the cool of the valley, is a welcome relief.

Like many waterways in the area, Coups Creek's modern history has not been peaceful. In July 1972, a sewer trunk main was laid under Coups Creek as part of the North Head Outfall, which runs from Blacktown to Manly. Observers of the area noted the significant damage to the creek bed, not just of Coups Creek, but others in the area, and the subsequent influx of exotic weeds like Privet (*Ligustrum* spp.) and Lantana (*Lantana camara*) in the wake of the work.

An almost complete tour of the site can be undertaken by following the waterways. In the southeast of the site, the land starts behind the houses at Warwick Place, spreading in a ten-hectare triangle north and west to Fox Valley Road. The deep gullies where the tributaries run are lined with Cheesewood (*Glochidion ferdinandi*) rainforest, rising on the northern-facing slopes into grasstree woodland. A patch of Sydney Turpentine–Ironbark Forest, a Critically Endangered Ecological Community, stands at the north of this triangle, butting up against the backyards of houses on Fox Valley Road. Water moves slowly here, with little slope to hurry it along into the Lane Cove River.

The waterways move far more quickly in the land northwest of Fox Valley Road. At the top of the catchment, the creek starts in Hornsby Council land, snaking into the Wahroonga Estate. At this end of the creek is the Bush Roundabout, an intersection of several trails with a central island, where stands a large noticeboard with the Wahroonga Waterways Landcare logo, emblazoned upon it.

The other side of the creek features dense Coachwood (*Ceratopetalum apetalum*) rainforest with a carpet of ferns and curtains of slender vines. At the midway point of the creek, a wooden bridge crosses the water, surrounded by a proliferation of *Crinum* lilies. Crossing this bridge one way takes a walker to the San Hospital, and areas of the bushland such as the ephemeral Fox Falls and the log seats of the bush chapel. The other way culminates at the aged care village and a steep climb to Mount Pleasant Avenue.

A tributary flowing down from the hospital meets Coups Creek at the opposite bank, its rocky bed providing a place for young rainforest plants to sprout. Downstream and upslope are vantage points from which it is possible to look across the valley to low sandstone cliffs where beginner abseilers are sometimes shown the ropes. Somewhere near those rocky outcrops is rumoured to be the remains of a shack, a squatter's castle from the 1950s or 1960s. The stony slopes here mean the bush is denser with fewer trails, so proving the rumour true, or indeed, false, has been difficult. The steepness of this part of the bush provides a perfect example of a vegetation gradient – from the Coachwood-Grey Myrtle rainforest of the creek banks, a trail rises up through meadows of ferns, then sharply transitions into drier, scrubby Sandstone Gully Forest of the woodland variety.

The tributary that meets the creek on the opposite side has a very different nature, meandering down a wide slope that floods during storms. Regeneration efforts in this area have reduced much of the erosion and revealed enchanting little waterfalls and pools. One day this area will return to the sublime fern gully it once was, but for now, the work continues.

WATERWAY

The creek finally falls through Tall Sydney Sandstone Gully Forest into drainage tunnels that stretch under The Comenarra Parkway and emerges as the Lane Cove River on the other side. The water has now left the Wahroonga bushland and is part of Lane Cove National Park.

Country

Indigenous history and knowledge of the area has been almost entirely lost. The name 'Wahroonga' supposedly derives from an Indigenous word meaning 'our home', but no sources appear to indicate from which Indigenous language group. The language that was once spoken in the area is also unknown, 'Ku-ring-gai' or 'Guringai' being a catch-all term developed by white men in 1892 and applied to Indigenous peoples from the Macleay River to south of Sydney. Studies by the Aboriginal Heritage Office have disproved that such a 'tribe' existed. This knowledge is sadly likely to be permanently extinguished.

There is, or rather was, one Indigenous site in the bushland, an unremarkable-looking overhang like many others through the valley, and indeed, providing less shelter than many others. However, a survey of the site noted two quartz fragments and a bone shard amongst the soil. In a kind of sad analogue, those items are now also gone.

White timber-getters began moving through the area along what is now Fox Valley Road in the early 1800s, logging all the timber they could find until management of timber getting was finally brought into check, although it was too late for many species. Hundreds of years later, the bush still does not see the diversity and scale of trees it once did.

The major lessee of the land around this time was Thomas Hyndes, who owned over 800ha of land in the Fox Valley area. As the timber-getters ran out of material, industry became more focused on orchards. The land was gradually divided and sold to various landholders, with much of the land which now forms the remaining Wahroonga bush going to John Brown. Many of the nearby streets, like Ada and Lucinda Avenues, are named after his children.

In 1857, a survey of the area identified a squatter family with an established peach orchard hidden in the rainforest valley near what is now Warwick Place, Wahroonga. The Coups family was likely brewing illicit cider with the peaches, a relatively common enterprise. It is after this family that Coups Creek, which runs through the Wahroonga bush and into the Lane Cove River, is named.

In 1903, the Sydney Sanitarium was opened in the Wahroonga Estate. It was a health retreat, complete with orchards, vegetable plots and a dairy, the latter of which has left traces of its existence in the form of a few rotting stakes and coils of barbed wire in the southern corner of the environmental conservation zone. It was redeveloped in 1973 as a medical facility, the San Hospital.

In 1927, plans were made to transform the Fox Valley ridgetop area into a model suburb, 'The Crown of Wahroonga'. These plans included the development of a significant road, which was never completed. The remains of the beginning of the cobblestone road can still be found only a few hundred metres outside of the boundaries of the Wahroonga bush. Where bush now stands, it will remain standing so long as the environmental conservation zone is in place. No more development will occur.

Above: Bleeding Heart leaves float in Coups Creek. Below: Smoke filters through the bush during a hazard reduction burn.

Left: A foggy morning in the valley.

Right: Walkers dwarfed by sandstone cliffs beside Coups Creek.

LAND

Fauna

A male Satin Bowerbird inspects his bower.

FAUNA

Fur

I will start with the creatures most people think of when hearing the term 'fauna'. The fluffy, warm-blooded animals that dart through the trees or the shrubbery and trick you into thinking they are supremely cuddly.

Having been on the receiving end of a Ringtail Possum (*Pseudocheirus peregrinus*) bite – through a thick gardening glove, I might add – I can confirm that they are much fiercer than they appear, especially when they feel threatened.

In 2016, I arranged for Fire and Rescue NSW to conduct a hazard reduction burn in the bushland south-east of Fox Valley Road. Burns are vital for the health and safety of an area. Indigenous people carried them out with confidence and skill, encouraging regrowth in stagnating areas. With the more sedentary lifestyles of people now living in the area, the idea of burning nearby vegetation is somewhat unnerving.

This particular burn was held at the beginning of autumn. Young animals have fledged or been weaned by this time, and the pace of plant growth is slowing in preparation for winter. Temperatures are falling. It is a good time for a hazard reduction burn.

We were all in position. The fire had reached about halfway down the slope when a small, snuffling creature emerged from the smoke at the bottom of the hill. Hot and finding breathing difficult, it stumbled across the fire crew at the lower handline, a member of which picked it up and offered it water before setting it on its way into deeper bushland away from the fire. It was our first, official sighting of a live, healthy, Long-nosed Bandicoot (*Perameles nasuta*), and we have not seen a living one since. This came after years of identifying bandicoot scratchings, conical holes dug in the soil beside the walking trails where they hunted for insects, and finding dead or dying specimens. Once a very old bandicoot came hopping out of the bush, right up to the area where the bush regenerators gathered to have lunch, and died at the feet of one of the staff. We knew they were there; finding healthy live examples was the difficult part.

Similarly, it was only when an arborist pointed out some seemingly nondescript scarring on our Red Bloodwood trees (*Corymbia gummifera*) that we discovered we had Sugar Gliders (*Petaurus breviceps*). These little marsupials chew into the sap-producing bark of Bloodwoods in distinct bands, feeding communally as family groups on the same tree for years until the bark becomes too scarred, and then move on to the next tree. For this reason, in stands of Bloodwoods, some trees may be ringed with these tapping bands, whilst their neighbours are completely untouched. Sugar Gliders are small and nocturnal, and despite camera traps, we have yet to see even a glimpse of their grey fur.

Common Brushtail Possums (*Trichosurus vulpecula*) and Common Ringtail Possums are, as their names suggest, more common and have been easier to spot. One 'Brushie' was found by the same arborist who noticed the Sugar Glider tapping bands; whilst climbing a dead tree with a colleague to assess the possibility of installing an artificial hollow, he came across a pre-existing hollow complete with a surprised, full-grown Brushtail Possum. The largest of all Australian possums, the Brushie is a meaty character with a prehensile tail and is a regular visitor to suburban and rural attics, much to many a homeowner's annoyance.

'Ringies' tend to be found in the Wahroonga bush under more unfortunate circumstances. Although they can be easily spotted at night, these smaller possums are usually visible by day in pieces, courtesy of the resident family of Powerful Owls (*Ninox strenua*). Occasionally they provide comfortable cushions for these owls, their white-tipped tails dangling out from beneath a feathered posterior. Some of their skulls, unearthed during forays into the bush, are now displayed in an education kit along with those of other animals.

What does this lack of visible fauna say? Is this a failure of the conservation aims of this patch of bushland? Is the effect of the surrounding humanity too pervasive? It certainly causes disappointment in some visitors who expect the bushland to resemble a zoo, or a scene from a nature documentary, where animals are easily visible and always present. This says more about their views of nature than the conservation efforts; the environment, whilst it can be entertaining, does not exist for the sole purpose of entertaining humanity. Wild animals do not lurk in the wings, waiting for their cue to enter, which anyone who has watched the 'behind the scenes' of any nature documentary will know. It may take months or even years of patience, dedication and disappointment before a single moment of interest is observed. Not a very attractive proposition for those who demand instant gratification.

On the other hand, it does also indicate the extent of human impact. Whilst this patch (or more accurately, these two patches) of bushland in Wahroonga covers a total of 31.4ha, this is a very small range for many species (as evidenced by the lack of macropods – such as kangaroos and wallabies – for example). Habitat fragmentation is considered one of the leading causes of biodiversity loss world-wide, and the solutions are not as simple as revegetating cleared areas or replacing exotic flora with native species. For some fauna, once habitat is cleared, they will not return despite the best rehabilitation efforts. On the other hand, some species have found exotic vegetation to be better habitat than native flora so, once changes have occurred, they may be irreversible.

In addition, the importation and subsequent lack of control of non-native animals is a significant problem. As much as I love cats, they are well-known killers of wildlife. It was common to come across the headless carcass of some otherwise intact bird in the bush – the *modus operandi* of the cat. The head is removed first, effectively immobilising and killing the prey, before the cat decides whether or not it actually cares to eat its victim.

Human impacts have reached far down the food web to organisms that have not yet even been identified, so small and obscure are they. These creatures make up the bulk of the kingdom Animalia, yet they are often overlooked. I am referring, of course, to insects and arthropods.

The Tiny

There is a particularly unusual set of residents in the bush. They are strangely wide for the type of creature they are, sausage-coloured and remarkably muscular, like the bodybuilders of the undergrowth. Touch them, and they can rapidly contract themselves down to half their size… and then squirt a watery fluid up to twenty centimetres into the air through pores in their skin.

The Frankfurter or Squirter Earthworm (*Didymogaster sylvaticus*) is somewhat alarming on the first encounter, with a body as thick and slightly longer than an adult finger and their predilection for squirting internal fluids. One's first instinct upon finding a squirter worm should be to rapidly cover it back up again with the shovelful of earth that had just been lifted off it. So of course my colleagues and I gathered up all of the specimens we had unearthed for a closer look. When they simply curled up even more, we decided to leave the poor creatures in peace. Worms are invaluable recyclers of waste, improvers of soil health, and nutritious food for many species. They can accelerate rehabilitation of degraded places, making them a bush regenerator's best friend. I like to show my appreciation for the work of earthworms by rescuing them when they are washed out by rain or mobbed by ants – the least I can do for such industrious workers.

The bush is filled with little gems. There are colourful, jewel-like Trapezoid Spiders (*Sidymella* spp.) that hide nervously in long lush grass and raise a tiny pair of tremulous legs when you stop to take a photo of them. Trapezoid Spiders have been spotted in many guises, from fawn-coloured individuals hiding in leaf litter, to bright green ones in the young grass, or straw-yellow in dead grass. Similarly-neon leaf-hopping Flatids (*Metcalfa* spp.) flit about as you disturb the grass. Only a few centimetres away might sit an Ogre-faced Spider (family Deinopidae), a fuzzy character with big black eyes that are somewhat bizarrely endearing, unless you are an arachnophobe. It was a regular occurrence when moving metal star-stakes to come across a broody mother Huntsman Spider (family

Sparassidae). Star-stakes are commonly used to mark monitoring points or as posts in simple fences in the Wahroonga bush, and these are often topped with plastic yellow caps to make them more conspicuous. Female Huntsman Spiders have discovered they are an excellent place to hide with an egg-sac, at least until some inconsiderate human turns up to move the stake. We learnt to gingerly lift the cap from the stake and carefully place it on the ground, upside down, to see if there were any occupants.

One morning I scooped an attractive lime green moth sitting in the middle of the carpark at work. It was about seven centimetres long, and with an apparent lack of care, sat on my hand as I carried it through the administrative building to a sunny spot in the gardens where I could deposit it. By the time I had encouraged it off my hand, it had decided, for some reason, to lay ten miniscule eggs on my palm, pale cream and each small as a pinhead. I later found out that this moth was *Aenetus scotti*, which despite its beautiful appearance, lacks a common name. This is the case with so many small and inconspicuous living creatures world-wide. People are fascinated by 'charismatic megafauna' – they want pandas and horses and dolphins – and miss the subtle and surprising beauty of the small.

My first encounter with the *Aenetus* genus did have a common name – the Splendid Ghost Moth (*Aenetus ligniverens*). Splendid it was, and so strange that for a long time afterwards, I was not entirely certain that the creature was a moth. I came across it on one of my bush patrols, ambling down a sloping trail with a critical eye on the invasive Kahili Ginger-lily (*Hedychium gardnerianum*) that was popping up everywhere and resisted the hacking of machetes and rapid application of Roundup Biactive. On one such plant, there perched an unusual little character.

This Splendid Ghost Moth gentleman, as I later discovered him to be, was about five or six centimetres long, and decked out in a green-white-brown camouflage pattern. His six fluffy legs, so unlike the usual spindly limbs seen on members of the Lepidoptera family, were gathered together above his head so that the majority of his body hung below the ginger stem. His body itself was also a curious shape, as if the camouflage outfit, fluffy legs and giant brown eyes were not strange enough. My first thought, seeing him, was of a picture frame holder, one of those small L-shaped stands that can be used to prop up pictures on a tabletop.

I took several photos of this amazing moth and spent a few weeks trying to identify it. His shape, legs, and apparent lack of antennae had me confused, and in the end I turned to some experts who confirmed that, yes, this was a moth. My discovery of *Aenetus scotti* cemented the *Aenetus* genus as my favourite group of moths, knocking Hawkmoths (Sphingidae family) from their long-held position.

On the subject of the small creatures that wander through the leaf litter, I identified at least six different species of ant in that patch of bush, from the angular and human-shy Spider Ants (*Leptomyrmex* sp.), to the one-and-a-half centimetres long and aggressive Jumper Ants (*Myrmecia nigrocincta*) that will jump up to ten centimetres towards a person with no hesitation (and perhaps with a hint of sadistic pleasure).

Jumper Ants are a large ant of the bulldog variety, with large pincers, black-red-black-red-black banding along the body and an aggressive attitude. They also have a nasty venomous sting that may produce an allergic reaction. I have had the misfortune of being stung on three different occasions by the Jumper Ant – on the last instance, the sting site on my leg swelled to twelve centimetres in diameter, with a hard, painful centre roughly five centimetres across. When first bitten, I could feel the venom travelling through my lymph system, causing sharp pain at the nodes in my groin and armpit and giving me a sore throat. For days, the burning, itching and stabbing pain in my leg made sleeping difficult and left a circular brown scar after the swelling finally went down, as well as a healthy respect for these fierce critters.

It was a common occurrence for a bush regenerator to transform from a focused weed destroyer to a hopping, yelling sprinter after accidentally treading on a nest of these ants.

Reactions varied on this theme; some workers would take longer than others to react, with one volunteer standing rigid with fear as ants liberally leapt up and down his body. Others feel the first sting and immediately know the drill – *run*.

Whatever your opinion is on the creepy-crawly, there is no doubt that their place in the world is vital. One of the big stories of 2016 – 2017 was the alarming rates of bee deaths in the world. The finger has been pointed variously at fungal infections, chemical biocides, and improper care by the beekeepers themselves. Whatever the cause, the fact remains that the global bee population is diminishing. In an anthropocentric light this is hugely problematic since around one third of crops rely on bee pollination to fruit. On an ecological scale, the extent of the eventual disaster is unknown – hundreds of thousands of flowering plants rely on bees and their pollinating services for survival.

Still, you might ask, what is the point of an insect like the mosquito? The mosquito seems to only serve as a blood drinker and a spreader of diseases (malaria kills two hundred million people worldwide every year) and to whine in your ear when you are trying to sleep.

Aside from these three things, mosquitoes are a great food source for all manner of insectivorous amphibians, reptiles, microbats and fish. More intriguingly, the mosquito is a pollinator for some of the tiniest of the native Australian orchids, those with flowers scarcely larger than a person's little fingernail. And if it is any consolation, of the three thousand-five hundred identified species of mosquito, only two hundred or so species actually bite humans.

More pleasant are the early morning walks in spring along Coups Creek. A mantis may suddenly appear on your arm, swaying like a martial arts master preparing to engage in battle. Steelblue Ladybeetles (*Halmus chalybeus*) are occasionally observed between sightings of more conventional orange and yellow ladybeetles with anywhere between three to twenty-three black spots. Damselflies and dragonflies of various colours and sizes scatter in all directions, flashing blue and red and yellow. Occasionally, a large one, wingspan as big as my palm, will hold still long enough to have its picture taken. One of the best photos I have taken by the creek is a detailed close-up of a female Blue-spotted Hawker (*Adversaechna brevistyla*), gauzy wings spread, bold cream geometric shapes along the length of her chocolate brown body.

Here today, gone the next, insects and arachnids usually have very short lifespans. The Splendid Ghost Moth, the Blue-spotted Hawker, the tiny eye-popping Trapezoid Spiders and icy blue and green Flatids that I saw will already be long gone. Their lives flicker in and out of existence rapidly and others take their place just as quickly.

What have we, humans, done for them, except make their short lives more difficult? In the gardens around the bush, we encouraged residents and workers to avoid using slug and snail pellets – not only were these killing integral parts of the ecosystem, they were causing secondary poisoning effects on the creatures that preyed on them.

Feathers

The most commonly sighted group of animals in the Wahroonga bushland by far is the birds. Birds of all kinds take advantage of the dense bush and abundant hollows, and sometimes even the soft hearts of nearby residents who sneakily feed them, despite our advice to the contrary. There are King Parrots (*Alisterus scapularis*) and Rainbow Lorikeets (*Trichoglossus molucannus*) and Crimson Rosellas (*Platycercus elegans*) whose whistles and chirrups make the trees sing. Sulphur-crested Cockatoos (*Cacatua galerita*), the delinquents of the bird world, merrily strip bottlebrushes of their flowers and hang upside-down from the tallest trees, yellow crests dramatically spread into mohawks as they screech raucously.

Daintier and less visible are the little Fairy- and Scrub-wrens, robins and finches that dart through the bracken (*Pteridium esculentum*) meadows. Eastern Yellow Robins (*Eopsaltria australis*), Spotted Pardalotes (*Pardalotus punctatus*), Silvereyes (*Zosterops lateralis*) and the occasional orange-blue-white of a male Variegated Fairy-wren (*Malurus lamberti*), which adorns the Wahroonga Waterway Landcare logo, halt bush regenerators in their tracks, leading to a scramble for phones to capture the rare moment. We were usually not fast enough.

The major celebrity is a male Satin Bowerbird (*Ptilonorhynchus violaceus*) who has set up court in a dense thicket of Small-leaved Privet (*Ligustrum sinense*) essentially ensuring that patch of exotic vegetation will not be removed any time soon. His favourite past-time is to sit in a tree near his bower and stare at human visitors with brilliant violet eyes. At times it is hard to tell who is the observer and who is the observed.

I have had the privilege of seeing him dance – first, a careful selection from his trove of collected bits-and-pieces that form the blue carpet to his bower. Then the display, waving the selected object (a bottle cap, part of a straw, a pen lid) aloft. Some hops, more waving, flaps of the wings. A posse of primary school students I have guided to the viewing spot pointed, gasped and chattered excitedly, as an appreciative audience should. The bird is magnificent and he knows it. Over nearly four years that I roamed the Wahroonga bush, he has attracted many a female and seen off several young upstart males, once facing three at one time, and you can still rely on him to always be available for a show.

The other famous inhabitants of the feathered variety are the Powerful Owls. As mentioned earlier, they tend to leave bits of their dinner lying about, unless they are sitting on it. Powerful Owls are the largest of Australia's owls at up to sixty-five centimetres from beak to tail tip, and are considered 'Threatened' in NSW. They have strangely small heads for owls, but retain the same slightly alarmed, rather grumpy expression.

My first sighting of one was by sheer chance. I'd heard about the owls from my colleagues during the first few months on the job, and also how rare it was to see them. And yet in the middle of my first year, hurrying along trails I still wasn't entirely familiar with, I came across a patch of 'whitewash' or pale bird droppings directly in the middle of the path. I stepped back (always a wise first move) and looked up.

A sleepy adult Powerful Owl scowled at me from the branches of a tall Turpentine Tree or *Yanderra* (*Syncarpia glomulifera*), unimpressed at being discovered. More lively was an immensely fluffy owlet, already almost as big as its parent, but still clad in snowy white down. It repeatedly performed the characteristic bobbing-swaying motion that owls do with their heads, an action that appears comical but has a very practical purpose. Owls' eyes are fixed, so unlike humans they can't look around without moving their heads. In order to get a good, three-dimensional idea of what they are looking at, owls therefore have to perform these acrobatic head dances.

This particular young owl bobbed and circled with its head, looking angry and alarmed simultaneously. The adult regarded me balefully with narrowed eyes before shutting them and turning away with apparent disgust at this nosy human.

Since then we have seen the owls many times in that particular tree. Sometimes it was two adults, sometimes a single adult, occasionally with a chick in tow. As owls cannot digest fur and bone, I have also found pellets under the tree, regurgitated balls of the indigestible parts of possums, rabbits, rats, and, if the claws are anything to go by, domestic cats. They make a convincing argument for keeping pet cats indoors.

They also make a good argument for slower and more careful driving. Two of us bush workers once found a pile of bones tangled in the thorny thicket of Lantana that provides a buffer against The Comenarra Parkway and a habitat for small birds. For half an hour, we carefully picked out progressively smaller and smaller bones, until we had in the bag between us the almost complete skeleton of a Powerful Owl, right down to its talons. This owl had not been attacked by another animal. No part of it had been eaten. Only a broken wing spoke of the moment a car had struck it and left it to die by the side of the road. I hope it died quickly. We passed the skeleton on to the Powerful Owl Project, a citizen science program run by Birdlife Australia that has sadly since been defunded.

On the other end of the scale are the smallest owls in Australia, the Southern Boobooks (*Ninox novaeseelandiae*). These thirty centimetres long and mostly dark brown owls wear perpetual scowls and are often described as angry flying feather-balls. We only saw these once in the Wahroonga bush, hiding out in the temperate rainforest by the sandstone cliffs in the south west of the land. One glare and they were gone.

The comedians of the bush are Brush Turkeys (*Alectura lathami*). Get too close and their attempts to move away become increasingly frantic and coupled with a gargling, gobbling noise. Intimidating as they may seem to the uninitiated, with their shocking red heads, yellow wattles and large black wings, they are easily cowed.

Brush Turkeys also have very odd ideas about parenting. They spend days raking up a massive pile of leaf litter in which to lay their eggs. Until the eggs hatch, the male diligently tests the temperature of the composting leaf pile to ensure conditions are optimal for the developing chicks, kicking away leaf matter or adding more as needed, to the chagrin of the owner of whichever carefully mulched backyard has been chosen. Although there is plenty of bushland around, Brush Turkeys prefer to choose nearby gardens for their gigantic nests.

Once the eggs have hatched however, the job of parenting ends. Brush Turkey chicks are 'precocious', that is, they can walk and feed themselves within minutes of hatching. It is common to see a round and fluffy brown turkey chick barrelling through the undergrowth or perched uncomfortably on very thin branches for a night's roost, completely alone, despite being around the size of a large grapefruit.

The first time I saw one sprinting alone through the managed gardens by the administrative buildings, my immediate instinct as a wildlife rescuer was to try and catch it to look after it. This was unnecessary, of course, and I soon became used to seeing fluffy little birds hurtling through the bushes.

Once, a few members of the bush team, myself included, came across a lone Brush Turkey chick as we walked along one of the trails. Unusually, it did not run away as we approached, and actually crept closer and closer through the ferns until it was finally standing at the edge of the trail. Then, suddenly, it flashed across the path, almost running across our shoes in the process. It disappeared into the ferns on the other side, popping its head up occasionally as it slowed back to a walk. Brush Turkeys will continue to be a source of entertainment.

The most commonly-seen feathered inhabitants are the Laughing Kookaburras (*Dacelo novaeguineae*). They follow the bush regeneration team in big family gangs, waiting for the opportunity to pounce on freshly overturned soil for insects and worms. Occasionally the whole mob will perch on a high branch and laugh raucously, an activity that has little to do with humour and everything to do with staking a territorial claim on a patch of bushland.

One kookaburra seemed unsatisfied by such meagre pickings as mere insects. At the edge of the bushland one day, reconnoitring a site for clean up, two of us spotted a kookaburra ambitiously beating a rat against a tree branch. Beating larger prey against a tree to stun or kill it is common kookaburra behaviour, but this rat was about half the size of the bird and possibly just as heavy, which is likely why during one particularly energetic bout of beating, the kookaburra dropped it.

I went over to inspect the rat. It was most definitely dead, so after taking a few photographs as evidence, I withdrew to allow the kookaburra to retrieve its meal, although how it was going to eat such a large rat, I was not sure. Occasionally I hear similar stories of kookaburras beating up rats, so they must have found some way of digesting them.

And then there are the frogmouths.

A local WIRES volunteer with a particular passion for Tawny Frogmouths (*Podargus strigoides*) successfully secured funding to build a rehabilitation aviary for her rescues. Frogmouths are very prone to disaster; their insectivorous diets have landed them into secondary poisoning from pesticides, and in front of cars as they pursue flying insects drawn by headlights at night. Additionally, their nests are little more than a few flimsy twigs, which with a slight breeze can be knocked to the ground with any eggs or chicks unfortunate enough to be perched inside. Finally, their characteristic log pose is their only defence. When in danger, frogmouths arrange their amazing wood-like plumage and elongate their bodies to resemble a jagged branch. They have no talons, unlike raptors, so all they can do is sit and wait, hoping to remain unseen.

The rescuer approached us with a proposal to build the rescue aviary on the grounds of the administrative buildings at the edge of the bushland. It was not a hard sell. The ten by six metre aviary went up within a few months and sixteen tawnies were introduced to their new quarters. The population since then has been in constant rotation as birds are rehabilitated and released back into the bush. Some are too badly hurt to be returned to the wild, such as Nela, blind in one eye and the matriarch of the group, taking newly-arrived youngsters under her wing. Others with brain damage from poisoning also remain.

The aviary is a favourite with walking groups and schools. Everyone competes to spot the most birds or watches avidly during meal times. Food was usually a dead mouse or a wriggling superworm shoved down their throat, but to keep them in tune with their natural food sources, the occasional large wild bush roach would help.

On one of the days I was hunting for roaches, I decided to roll over the logs that lined the edges of one of the bush trails. When rolling logs, it is important to roll them towards your body, so that anything potentially dangerous (spiders, snakes) will make their escape in the other direction (away from you). I rolled a log, gathered a few large and juicy bush roaches and dropped them in a bucket with some leaf litter before returning the log to its original position.

Something wriggled in the disturbed leaf litter.

Cold Blood

Several thoughts jumped into my head at once. This thing, whatever it was, was tiny. If it was a snake, it would be very young. However, its wriggling seemed incredibly ineffective for a snake. It was taking precious seconds to burrow into the leaf litter, and its whole movement and appearance eventually seemed to me so unlike a snake's that I finally reached down and picked it up.

It turned out to be a skink. A very long tailed skink with tiny weak legs that did nothing but dangle by its sides as it tried to wriggle free from my hand. I took photos, as usual, then tucked the skink under a dead leaf by the log.

I later identified the skink as an Earless Three-toed Eastern Skink (*Hemiergis talbingoensis*) and became increasingly aware of how common they were on site. Disturbing leaf litter or rolling logs could send dozens of them wriggling frantically for cover. They are an interesting example of how evolution works, representing the in-between stages where legs become increasingly useless. Yet it struck me how bad they are at wriggling! For some reason this was their chosen form of locomotion, and it had to be working for them to still be present in such abundance. Sometimes nature does not seem to make much sense.

Take the Golden Crown Snake (*Cacophis squamulosus*) for example. These little snakes cropped up occasionally in the Wahroonga bushland (again under logs), slim and dark in appearance. They are fairly venomous, yet they show a tendency to defend themselves by headbutting their perceived attacker. I have yet to see this unusual defensive display, but then I am not the type to rudely harass a snake. In my opinion, the best policy, with any wild animal, is generally to leave it alone.

Not so with one of my colleagues. He would grab every Blue-tongued Lizard (*Tiliqua tiliqua*) he saw and give it a thorough checking over for ticks. Several times I would be sitting in the office writing reports only for him to burst through the door triumphantly brandishing a lizard and calling for tweezers, and I would spend the next half hour carefully extracting ticks from the poor Blue-tongue's ears.

He would chase Eastern Water Dragons (*Intellegama lesueuri*) for a similar treatment. The year before I began working at the site, he found an adult Diamond Python (*Morelia spilota spilota*) on one of the lawns and proceeded to have his photo taken with it cradled carefully in his arms and across his shoulders. The snake seemed immune to his affections, however, and slipped away into the bush as soon as it was released some distance away from the lawn.

One of the best encounters involving reptiles occurred in the spring of 2015. A team of us were clearing Trad (*Tradescantia fluminensis*) from the banks of the creek, enjoying the spring warmth and the quiet trickle of water. I tore away a clump of Trad to find a cache of very small white eggs nestled in a shallow depression in the soil. They were almost identical to the native finch egg in size, colour and shape, but their texture gave them away – leathery and tough, rather than hard and brittle. The team gathered briefly to admire the clutch and then went back to work. And found another nest.

And another.

And another, until it seemed the whole creek bank was lined with tiny skink nests and I found myself gingerly tiptoeing around, wincing at the mental image of tiny crushed eggs. You come across life in the most unexpected of places.

There is one skink that as yet eludes identification. Amongst the Eastern Water Skinks (*Eulamprus quoyii*), Common Garden Skinks (*Lampropholis guichenoti*) and Delicate Skink (*Lampropholis delicata*) is a small grey lizard with an orange-red tail, although not so bright as that of the Lined Fire-tailed Skink (*Morethia ruficaudata*) of north-western Australia. It resembles much more closely the Red-tailed Litter-skink (*Lygisaurus malleolus*) of Queensland, and could be a red-tailed form of the South-eastern Slider (*Lerista bougainvillii*), but descriptions of the small skink species are lacking, so it is difficult to be certain, especially since they would only appear rarely and usually amongst a jumbled pile of plant pots in one of our plant nurseries.

There are also geckos. I was taking a shortcut through the bush, walking through a patch known to the bush regenerators as 'Weed Heaven' (the name is self-explanatory). As I was almost at the top of the ridge, I noticed a Small-leaved Privet practically growing on bare sandstone and made the incorrect assumption that it would be easy to remove.

No sooner had I started tugging at an epiphytic root then a large sheet of sandstone sloughed off, narrowly missing my foot and exposing two very small, stunned creatures. One was a cryptically-patterned Southern Leaf-tailed Gecko (*Platycercus phyllurus*) that had lost its tail sometime prior, although at first I thought my disastrous privet-removing attempts had done the deed. The second was a dark brown Bibron's Toadlet (*Pseudophryne bibronii*) that sat so still and curled up that I thought it had died of shock. I had to nervously prod it a few times before it moved and reassured me that it was, in fact, alive. In spite of all this, I was not able to remove the privet, in the end.

Since then I have kept an eye and an ear out for the frogs of the bush. The ever-changing Peron's Tree Frog (*Litoria peronii*), with skin that changes colour at will, but is always recognisable by its unique, cross-shaped pupil. The Striped Marsh Frog (*Limnodynastes peronii*) has a call like the sound of a knock on timber. Whenever I heard them whilst crossing a wooden bridge, I would look around to see if someone was following me. The Eastern Dwarf Tree Frog (*Litoria fallax*) has a higher-pitched creaking call, although we tend to see it more often than we hear it, crouched on a bank of Coups Creek or a low-lying basin amongst damp vegetation. In spring, the creek and tributaries are frothy with frogspawn, a pure white foam speckled with black dots that slowly disappears only to be replaced by another.

There is one group of animals that made their home in the Wahroonga bush that I have not yet discussed. We have had birds and arthropods, worms and mammals, reptiles and amphibians. The creek is small but supports so much life, although several of its own tributaries are ephemeral. Unless there is heavy, sustained rainfall, the creek water does not run in an unbroken rush into the Lane Cove River.

And yet, one day in spring of 2015, with the creek water a little higher than usual due to some heavy rain a few days prior, I was crossing the creek when something made a tremendous splash just ahead of me.

It was an eel.

The discovery was cause for a lot of excitement amongst the bush team, and a lot of head-scratching as to how it had made its way up the river, through the drainage tunnels that run under The Comenarra Parkway, and then over the concrete spillway where Coups Creek meets the Lane Cove River. Has it somehow swum against the surging current as the rainwater poured in? Had it *climbed* its way upstream? However it had made its way, it must have been a bold and intrepid eel indeed, since we have only ever seen one more since.

Another time, some of the team were crossing the only bridge over Coups Creek when something small darted through the water. And then another. And another. Eventually we were able to make out, in the tannin-stained water, small fish shooting forwards and freezing among the rocks. We quickly scrambled down the bank to the rocky creek bed to take a closer look.

They seemed to be fairly nondescript little fish, but any fish was an unusual sight in Coups Creek, and this was the first time we had seen these characters. These were Cox's Gudgeon (*Gobiomorphus coxii*) a native species that when young and small find safety in remoter upper reaches of river systems by swivelling their fins and using them like suction cups to climb flat vertical surfaces where only a trickle of water runs. As adults up to 19cm long, they are far too large to climb but can safely return to the larger rivers.

Casual visitors to the valley are keen to see its animals, the birds and the mammals particularly. But there is more beyond the animals that live in this bushland. They are only a part, a small part, of a community of personalities. It is time to introduce you to some plants.

Clockwise from above left: Peron's Tree Frog, Aenetus scotti, *a male King Parrot preening.*

Above: A Diamond Python in a tree. Below (L-R): A Tawny Frogmouth in characteristic log pose; a rare sight – a Ringtail Possum in daylight.

Flora

*Spotted Sun Orchid (*Thelymitra ixioides*)*

FLORA

Canopy

Amongst the many photos we have taken during walks through the bush, my supervisor has one particular favourite. It is a shot of a group of local school children gathered around an old Sydney Red Gum (*Angophora costata*), hands linked to embrace the tree. It is not entirely clear from the photo, but at least ten children are in the hug. At easily a hundred years old, this tree has reached an impressive size, dwarfing anything else nearby.

Trees tend to grow slowly. And because they grow slowly, if we allow them, they grow huge.

Smaller plants have more of a smash-and-grab approach. They grow quickly, taking advantage of whatever sunlight, nutrients and water they can get so they can reproduce and repeat the cycle.

Fungi, those strange structures that are not plants but in an entire Kingdom of their own, appear where there is decaying matter and moisture. They are therefore prolific in autumn and always make an impressive display in a striking range of colours.

Descriptions of vegetation types always start from the top, with the dominant tree species. Sydney Red Gums are a particular favourite of mine. Their planished limbs and trunks curl and twist in contortionist and distinctive ways. A staff of Angophora wood stands in my bedroom, its twists and knots immediately calling to mind a dragon's head, like those carved into the prows of Viking ships. Polished, it leans against the wall and glares at anyone who dares to enter the room. A bowl of Angophora bark, carefully sealed and presented to me as a gift from a local preschool that I walked through the bush many times, lies nearby, holding small treasures from the site – bones, petrified wood, stones, fruits, feathers.

Every year, the outer layers of their trunks dry, harden, and fall away, leaving the tree shining white and renewed. Unfortunately, this smooth whiteness makes them a target for vandals. It is not uncommon to come across Red Gums that had been carved with initials or words, or even some that had been tagged with spray paint. Since the bark sheds every year, these occurrences tend to be a source of amusement rather than anything else, if occasionally underscored with a sense of disappointment and unease at these examples of disrespect to our providers of oxygen. At the same time it is sometimes darkly whispered that any couple that has their names carved into a tree is cursed to have a failed relationship.

Off-trail stands an old Red Gum that I came across one day in pursuit of a bird. Circling the trunk, I noticed several groups of long nails, all in threes, hammered into the trunk, starting from my shoulder height and ending several metres up at the lowest branch. Clearly these nails had been inserted to facilitate climbing, and from the bark layers clinging to the nails from the Angophora's annual renewal of its skin, the nails had been there for over a decade. The tree was still very much alive, apparently unperturbed by this intrusion.

The most numerous trees in the Wahroonga woodlands are Blackbutts (*Eucalyptus pilularis*) and Turpentines. The former have rough bark that spreads from the ground to the first branch, then bare limbs beyond. Turpentines are rough and crumbly all over and have unusual fused fruits. Both have popularity in the timber industry due to their resistance to insects, Blackbutts having uses such as cladding and decking, whilst the Turpentine, difficult to ignite and very durable, has been used to build wharves. It has been over a hundred years since logging occurred in the Wahroonga bush, yet the Blackbutts and Turpentines are still relatively small and dense. However, without them, the valley would be very bare.

To the north-east of the site are the Sydney Blue Gums (*Eucalyptus saligna*). Their white, straight trunks, unlike the Red Gum, have a distinctly blue tinge, and a low sock of rough brown bark clings to their base. Blue Gum High Forest, the ecological community they lend their name to, is critically endangered, and recognised as such by both NSW and Federal laws.

Creeping up from south of Sydney have come the Illawarra Flame Trees (*Brachychiton acerifolium*). With huge palmate leaves that shed to reveal burning red flowers, the Flame Tree produces a mixed response among nature lovers in the Sydney Basin. On the one hand, the striking incandescent blossoms, free of leaves, make an amazing sight, a flaming cascade against the cool green of the lush forest in which they grow. On the other, Illawarra Flame Trees, as their name suggests, originated in the Illawarra region and have been creeping northwards, to the annoyance of those trying to preserve Sydney's bush in the moment. Is such a thing possible? Is it right? The debate that rages between preservation of ecosystems as is and controlled transition is a bitter one that the Flame Tree is only one face of.

By contrast, the tall and prized Red Cedar (*Toona ciliata*) is no longer a common sight in the sandstone gullies where they were once numerous. Logging in the nineteenth century removed the giants, and the Cedar Moth (*Leptocneria reducta*) made sure they didn't come back, their larvae feeding on the growing tips of young cedars, effectively killing the plant. A few adolescent specimens remain in the Coups Creek valley, not saplings, but neither are they the huge organisms that once stretched through the valley.

In any case, I find the trees a soothing presence. One of the best parts of the job was pausing from weeding or planting or moving rocks for a moment, taking off the gloves and letting my overheating hands cool against the bark of the tree beside me. In these quiet moments, I would let recognition of the age of the tree wash over me as the throbbing in my hands receded. I would let it remind me why I was there, why I had chosen the environment as my calling, and then I would pull the gloves on again and get back to work.

Understorey

Another of the highlights of the job was sampling the local bush tucker. Identifying what was edible was one of the first things I learnt when I began my work. During morning tea and lunch breaks, I would wander along the trails with a field guide, or a bush tucker website open on my phone, examining each plant. I learnt to look for the tiny neon berries of the Native Currant (*Leptomeria acida*), the distinctive three-veined leaves of the Native Sarsaparilla (*Smilax glyciphylla*) and the more non-descript, savoury leaves of the Grey Myrtle (*Backhousia myrtifolia*). I learnt that unripe Geebungs (*Persoonia* spp.) suck all the moisture from your mouth as soon as you try to eat them and are therefore best picked purple and scattered beneath the plant they dropped from. The ripe berries of the Native Coffee Bush (*Breynia oblongifolia*) and Flax-lily (*Dianella* spp.) are small but intensely sweet. Native Raspberry (*Rubus parvifolius*) is prickly-leaved but the berries are delicious, although unlike their European namesakes. Wombat Berry (*Eustrephus latifolius*), Sandpaper Fig (*Ficus coronatus*) and Lilly-pilly (*Acmena* spp. and *Syzygium* spp.) all bear tasty fruit, whilst the native orchids have tiny, tasteless and starchy tubers.

As a caveat, whilst gathering and eating bush tucker is great fun, it can also be a risky business. Australia hosts many poisonous plants, and even some 'edible' vegetation that requires specific preparations in order to be safely eaten. Kangaroo Apple (*Solanum aviculare*), for example, grows abundantly in the valley, to the point where there is a healthy 'orchard' of the plant high above the south bank of Coups Creek. As a member of the Solanaceae family, Kangaroo Apple is related to some of our most commonly eaten foods – tomatoes, potatoes, capsicum, aubergine and the like. However, it is also cousin to Deadly Nightshade (*Atropa belladonna*) and Mandrakes (*Mandragora* spp.), some of the most poisonous plants in existence. It is unsurprising then that Kangaroo Apples are only to be eaten when vivid orange-red, and even so, contains the chemical solasidine, which is commercially harvested from the plant in some countries to create a contraceptive. There are stories that Indigenous peoples used Kangaroo Apple as such.

Further, some inedible species so closely resemble edible plants that unless the harvester is absolutely certain of identity of the potential morsel that they are looking at, it is more prudent to err on the side of caution and leave it alone. Native Sarsaparilla can sometimes look very similar to the non-edible but closely related Lawyer Vine (*Smilax australis*). Wombat Berry and Scrambling Lily (*Geitonoplesium cymosum*) are very similar in appearance until they produce fruit; the former bearing bright orange berries, and the latter, black.

Aside from bush tucker, the shrub layer provides vital habitat for the small birds that flit about the valley. Small bird habitat is in low supply within urban areas, although some species have taken advantage of hedgerows. Development has fragmented dense understorey communities, and forced small birds to either seek alternatives, or leave all together. As a result, dense weeds such as Lantana and Privet, invasive as they are, are excellent places for small birds to hide.

In the valley, Bracken, young Coachwood and Blackwattle (*Callicoma serratifolia*) give small birds a place to hide and nest. We have been lucky – a study in 2017 by researchers at the Centre for Biodiversity and Conservation Sciences at the University of Queensland found that removal of weed species, such as Lantana, and replacement with native species, can actually harm populations of small birds. When the habitat provided by the weeds is removed, the birds leave, and even if native alternatives are installed, they are unlikely to return. In spite of the mass removals of Privet, Lantana and Balloon Vine (*Cardiospermum grandiflorum*) throughout the Wahroonga Bush, enough habitat remained intact that when the native regeneration and revegetation emerged, the birds remained.

Groundcovers

At last count, there were twenty-three different native orchid species on site. Every year has brought one or two new species to light.

The smallest are the Pixie Caps (*Acianthus fornicatus*). First appears a heart-shaped leaf, small as a ten-cent coin. Then a narrow spike, rarely growing taller than ten centimetres in the Coups Creek area, topped off with a cluster of tiny translucent, pink-striped blossoms. They are so small that spotting them is more effectively achieved by looking for the leaves that thickly coat the forest floor rather than the flowers.

There are two *Dipodium* orchid species – the Slender Hyacinth (*Dipodium roseum*) and the Spotted Hyacinth (*Dipodium variegatum*), each bearing pink flowers with curled petals. These are some of the showier and more beautiful of the native orchids on the site, particularly the Spotted Hyacinth Orchid with its hot pink and snow white blotches.

Similarly attractive are the *Thelymitra* orchids, the Plain Sun Orchid (*Thelymitra nuda*) and the Spotted Sun Orchid (*Thelymitra ixioides*). These orchids are so named for their habit of only opening in direct sunlight. Both are a limpid blue, although the Spotted Sun Orchid bears multiple small dark spots like freckles across its petals.

A more recent discovery was the strangely-shaped Mayfly Orchid (*Acianthus caudatus*). Its petals have mutated into long red filaments that reach out perpendicular to the stem. In the spring of 2017, traipsing through the undergrowth in pursuit of a calling Brown Gerygone (*Gerygone mouki*), a group of us almost fell over a tiny patch of these orchids. I could not help sitting and pausing to savour the moment – golden spring sunlight filtering dappled through the trees, the smell of damp leaf litter, a tiny patch of Mayfly Orchids before me and the curiously-shaped upside-down teardrop of the Gerygone nest just above.

Native orchids of southeast Australia are mostly unlike the popular image of orchids. They are generally very small, with ephemeral leaves, if any. They rely on mycorrhizal fungi for nutrients, as their lack of substantial leaves means their capacity for photosynthesis is limited. To illustrate further the strangeness of native Australian orchids, the saga of the Dainty Bird Orchid (*Chiloglottis trapeziformis*) and the Ant Orchid (*Chiloglottis formicifera*) provides a great example.

As the Dainty Birds were emerging in 2017, photos of different *Chiloglottis* were beginning to appear on the various native plant enthusiast groups on social media. One particular set of photographs made me second-guess our identification of the Dainty Bird Orchid in the Wahroonga bush. Many *Chiloglottis* look very similar, with only the smallest of visible differences separating them.

I had available two photos, one from 2013, before I had started work at the site, and one from only a week before that I had personally taken. Someone in a Facebook group pointed out that the orchids in the two photos showed some differences. The 2013 flower bore tiny black warts on its lower 'lip' petal or labellum, whilst the 2017 orchid had a bare labellum.

After much to-ing and fro-ing as the online community weighed into the argument, it was eventually decided that the former photo showed an Ant Orchid, whilst the latter was a true Dainty Bird Orchid. To make things more confusing, both orchid species commonly grow together, although careful inspection of each flower after the discovery of the two species has only revealed Dainty Birds on site. The Ant Orchid has not been seen since.

Other stars of this fairyland setting are clusters of greenhoods (*Pterostylis* spp.) will often emerge suddenly from the fallen leaves like a stand of lanterns, delicate green lights on equally delicate green stems. The Nodding Greenhood (*Pterostylis nutans*) in particular has a pendulous single flowerhead and resembles a lamppost. Tall Greenhoods (*Pterostylis melagramma*) display best of all of this genus the 'trigger' that each flower contains. At the touch of an insect, a modified labellum flicks upwards, pushing the insect into the bloom's pollen sacs. This is not a carnivorous mechanism like that of the Venus Fly-trap (*Dionaea muscipula*); the only way out for the insect is to wriggle through the pollen, thus ensuring the plant's reproduction.

Autumn sets the stage for a major actor; fruiting fungal bodies pop up everywhere, capitalising on the cooler and wetter weather. What we usually call fungi the showy bit that sticks out above the ground or from a rotting log, is actually only the fruit. The body of the fungus lies under the ground, efficiently digesting the rotting organic matter it comes in contact with. This efficiency has made them excellent partners for symbiosis, hence their relationship with native orchids. The fungal tissue directly infiltrates the roots of the orchid, assisting the orchids growth by synthesising nutrients, and in return receiving carbon and soil moisture. Amongst the leaf litter, fungi in an amazing array of shapes and colours appear, from pale Earthstars (*Geastrum* spp.) to the nebula-like wheels of *Russula* fungi. Frequently, the vivid red of the Stinkhorn Anemone (*Aseroe rubra*) warns walkers of the terrible smell that accompanies it, long before it reaches our noses.

Best of all are the displays of brilliant blue Sky-blue Pinkgills (*Entoloma virescens*) and vibrant red Ruby Bonnets (*Mycena viscidocruenta*) that occasionally make an appearance together, lending a party-like atmosphere to the forest floor, or the eye-catching purple wheels of Mauve Waxgills (*Porpolomopsis lewellinae*) that burst from the damp leaf litter.

Fungi bring together ecosystems in such incredibly important ways, breaking down dead material and producing from it the nourishment so vital to the forest's survival. Their filaments spread throughout the soil, binding to the roots of plants, from the smallest orchids to the tallest Eucalypts. In this way, they are one of the greatest binding forces in the ecological community.

The work of Wahroonga Waterways Landcare has broadened the concept of community far beyond the plants and animals, water and soils, air and rocks. Interacting with that idea of a community is the more quickly recognised concept of human communities, in some ways separate and yet so deeply intertwined.

These entangled, separate-yet-not worlds ensure the survival of each other, earth meeting walking feet, air meeting written and spoken words, plants meeting working hands.

Community supports land, land supports life, life supports community.

Above: Ruby Bonnets and Sky-blue Pinkgills. Below: Dianella *flowers.*

Left: Wombat Berry

Right: A Dainty Bird Orchid.

FLORA

Community

Bush regenerators gather around one of the oldest trees on site, an Angophora

COMMUNITY

Words

Writing about Coups Creek and the surrounding bush have generally either been confined to government or management documents or the occasional passing reference in history or guide books of the greater Lane Cove River catchment, such as the STEP *Field Guide to the Bushland of the Lane Cove Valley*. There are a few blog posts, and even one or two poems. They are worth looking for online, but are understandably short on detail. This book, then, has been many years in the making. It is the most comprehensive collection of information on the Coups Creek bushland publicly available.

When I became coordinator of Wahroonga Waterways Landcare, I decided I wanted to write about the bushland and share it with the local community. I have two great loves in life – writing and nature – and in this way I could bring the two together. A small folder began to grow in my office cupboard – news articles, presentation posters, newsletter pieces, a paper on the Lane Cove Catchment. The folder next to it became stuffed with brochures, event calendars, small field guides and newsletters of our own.

A small piece on our Powerful Owls was picked up and expanded upon by the Daily Telegraph. Little snippets of the wonders in the valley were featured in STEP newsletters, in Regenevitas, newsletter of the Friends of Lane Cove National Park, in PAWS, newsletter of the Wildlife Land Trust, and the Hornsby Advocate.

To the National Landcare Conference in 2016 I brought an A3 poster summarising the results that had been achieved in the Wahroonga bushland over thirteen years, starting with the initial regeneration attempts in 2003. The right hand column of the poster reads:

COMMUNITY

Since 2003

11 hectares of weeds cleared

20 hectares rehabilitated

Landcare group commenced

100 volunteers

2 National Tree Days

(Over 200 plants)

6 school tree plantings

(Over 700 plants)

23 species of native orchids

40 native bird species

1 breeding pair of Powerful Owls

1 male Satin Bowerbird

Dozens of education tours for both adults and children

Partnerships with local groups

Permit for local National Park

Partnership with local council

Partnerships with schools

Talks at conferences

And as three years of funding from the Wildlife Land Trust came to a close, I wrote for PAWS:

"Vast swathes of privet and lantana were cleared to make way for fast growing natives such as Kangaroo Apple and Pittosporum. Giant Red Gums emerged from the dense jungle and native orchids peeped from the dense leaf litter until patches of the bush abounded with tiny flowers like sprinklings of stars."

The minutiae and the grandeur of the bushland inspire. From the star-like flowers at ground level to the soaring canopy and all the life in between, there is so much to write about that this book only covers a fraction. Take a walk through the bush and you will see why.

Walks

Some of my favourite days were those when we held educational tours. Many times I led groups of schools students, volunteers, or members of the public around the valley, pointing out flowers, bush tucker or birds. Their interest and delight in observing these sights always gave me a satisfied feeling of a job well done. From fungi spotting in autumn to year round orchid tours and early spring bush tucker tasting, there was always something to show the visitors.

We liked to coordinate these walks in conjunction with some sort of environmental event; Clean Up Australia Day, or National Tree Day, for example, would often see us cleaning up or planting early in the morning, followed by morning tea and a ramble through the bush. Participants ranged from entire preschool, primary school or secondary school classes, retirees, and bushwalking groups. One tour was held specifically for wildlife careers in the northern suburbs of Sydney, to assist them in identifying suitable natural food plants for the native animals they had rescued.

Sometimes we would have corporate volunteers. They always had good fun being out of the office, although some days were more memorable than others. During one of our corporate volunteer days, we decided to get the participants planting trees. As they completed the task, I gestured at the wooden stakes hammered into the ground next to each plant. "Could you all take the pots that the plants were in, and place them upside-down on the stakes?" Most of the volunteers complied, but one of the men, looking worried, repeated, "The pots?"

It had never occurred to me before that day that I would need to go through how to plant a tree, but in subsequent planting events, I always made sure to let the participants know that they had to take the plant out of the pot before putting it in the hole where it would live out its future.

One autumn, I organised a pilot night time walk. A small troop of participants with torches scanned the trees for wildlife as we followed the trails in the dark. It is easier at night to see how close the bush really is to suburbia. During the day, distant buildings blend with the trees, but at night their shining lights blaze through the canopy, startlingly near. An abundance of shining circles, the reflective eyes of Ringtail Possums, shone back at us as we circled the outermost trails of the valley. The deeper into the vegetation we travelled, the fewer eyes we saw, until they eventually disappeared. From then on, we only saw an eel and a tiny scorpion (*Lychus marmoreus*) that froze in our lights, then slowly attempted to shrink its body even further.

Very occasionally, we would leave the bush and take our show to a school. Whilst we preferred conducting tours in nature, where the participants can see, touch, smell, taste and hear the environment around them, it is not always possible for people to visit, particularly time-strapped school groups.

At these times we would gather up an array of realia – objects that the students could see and touch to give them a better sense of what we were talking about – and head over to a school in our khaki shirts, the little Variegated Fairy-wren logo sewn to the left shoulder and right breast. My wren sat a little jauntily as I had sewn the patch on late at night and not noticed the tilt. Still, I liked the little quirk and it was barely noticeable to anyone except me.

We would also bring pictures, to add to the visual impact. Humans are generally more receptive to visual cues than lecturing, so we would let the picture and realia do the talking – photos of colourful parrots and flowers, animal bones and feathers gathered from the bush, a picture of a Grey-headed Flying-fox (*Pteropus poliocephalus*), bush tucker we had harvested fresh that morning for the students (and their teachers) to try. We wanted them to experience nature as much as possible, even if they couldn't physically be there.

But best were the times when the students were out in the valley with us. They would watch the Satin Bowerbird dance, enthralled, or compete with each other to see who could eat the largest number of sour Native Currants in one go. A few of the more adventurous ones would inevitably fall into Coups Creek, scaring about five years off the lives of the supervising staff. Preschoolers would view everything with a mixture of confusion and benevolence, primary schoolers with eagerness, secondary schoolers feigning disinterest but unable to contain themselves when possum skulls were brought out, and tertiary students with the intensity of a dry sponge.

Each time, they learnt something new, and so did we.

Work

At a time when biodiversity laws in NSW are in a state of change and confusion, the work being achieved in the Wahroonga bushland is an important reminder to remain hopeful and remember the power of the grassroots.

To do good work, it helps to have good tools. Every bush regenerator has a kit that is variation on a basic theme. There is a surprising joy in having good tools to work with. When I was fortunate enough to be nominated for and to receive a prize as a 'Highly Commended Young Landcarer' in the Greater Sydney region in 2017, I used my award money to purchase some good quality trowels for the Landcare group. There was a great deal of excitement when I first presented these new tools to the bush team and volunteers, and the sense of satisfaction amongst them lasted for months; a regenerator would still pull out one of these with an approving look and some comment about how great they were.

Gloves can be tricky. My favoured pair is heavy duty, thick with rubber plates along the backs of the hands and fingers so that they resemble motorcycle gloves. They are very protective but become soggy quickly in damp or wet weather. More standard part-rubber gardening gloves deal better with wet conditions but are less protective and often end up in tatters after a few weeks of work. Occasionally I would wear fingerless bicycle gloves in situations where I needed to feel textures or grip better, but still wanted to protect the palm and back of my hand. Whatever the choice, gloves are essential for a bush regenerator. I once made the mistake of trying to yank out a Cunjevoi (*Alocasia brisbanensis*) that I thought was a taro plant (*Colocasia esculenta*) bare-handed, and discovered for myself that many members of the Araceae family have sap that contains calcium oxalate crystals. I could not wash it away and spent two hours feeling as though my hands were burning off. Lesson learnt. Wear gloves.

The particular piece of equipment that had all the bush team excited, although only a few of us carried them, were bush knives.

These portable multi-use tools could dig, cut, and lever, making them incredibly useful for bush regeneration work. The one I still use today is an intimidating character; having ordered it online, I was surprised and at first a little unnerved by the weight and size of the blade, but I quickly became used to both it and the reactions of startled onlookers.

One of my colleagues carried two knives, a small narrow blade more suited to piercing and scraping, and a broader one for digging, cutting, and levering. Using a narrow blade rather than a wide trowel creates less disturbance of soil, lowering the likelihood of erosion, protecting the roots of established native plants, and reducing the risk of weeds gaining a suitable space to seed and grow.

The most important thing about the work, though, was not the tools, but to have fun. Rolling through the bush in the all-terrain vehicle or the ute, I would dramatically hum the *Indiana Jones* theme song to give my colleagues a laugh. We would harvest and cook edible exotics we would find during our work, like tomatoes or potatoes. If we found toys dumped in the bush – a scooter, a soccer ball, a plush tiger – next moment we would be riding around trying to steer the scooter with its busted wheels, playing soccer, finding a comfortable spot in a work vehicle for the tiger to sit. Someone would turn up the radio in the ute to give us a soundtrack to work to.

This kind of enjoyment is all the more important given how much work we had to do. The land is managed under a Biodiversity Management Plan approved by the Federal Government, covering weeds, vegetation, fire, pests, water, soil, and habitat issues. Any work must be recorded and documented, following detailed schedules. The educational work conducted by Wahroonga Waterway Landcare is additional to this. It is hard but rewarding, giving back to a huge community of plants, animals, soils, biotic and abiotic neighbours, a world made of smaller worlds.

Worlds

There are communities in nature, communities in human society, vegetation communities, social communities, communities within communities, worlds within worlds. Nature writers have been trying to remind us that 'humanity' versus 'environment' is a false battle. Humans are part of nature, and all efforts to produce a 'safe, clinical space separate from the wild has only created a thin veneer to hide behind. Children provide the best examples of this. So many times I have presented to primary school students a natural curiosity, like an edible berry, or a gleaming Leopard Slug, and seen them turn away in fear. The younger the child, the more quickly they change their mind, and, hesitantly at first, but then more eagerly, reach out and take the strange wild thing that has been offered to them.

Over the years, that childlike wonder seems to have been suppressed at younger and younger ages. Five year olds shake their heads fearfully at the prospect of a Native Sarsaparilla leaf, or refuse to take off the gloves they were provided for a tree planting, until they are out of the bush. I cannot comment on the many factors that produce these responses. All I can say is that I have been startled each time, by the level of fear in the child and the profound sadness it evokes within me. The early to mid 2010s saw an academic interest in the benefits of direct contact between natural soils and the bare skin of the palms of the hands or the soles of the feet. Studies appear to have found health benefits from the practice as it raises dopamine levels, leading to lower stress levels and greater happiness. The sheer joy of nature, of seeing greenery, of feeling the soil, and smelling moisture on the air, is so very important, and people are missing out.

The disconnect is most apparent amongst the dog walkers.

The trails through the bush are popular with people who want to walk their pet dogs. Generally we were accepting of this, on the proviso that these dogs remained on a leash. There are some that comply with this simple request – and of course, some who do not.

Of these there are three kinds. The first are those who silently leash their dogs after being confronted. Some of these try very hard to ignore the bush worker in the fluorescent yellow shirt who is chasing after them and shouting, but eventually they comply, without a word. Typically these people unleash their dog again as soon as the bush worker is out of sight. On one occasion, driving through the bush in the all-terrain vehicle, I came across a man jogging with his unleashed dog. The dog bounced happily in front of the vehicle and I stopped, firstly to avoid running over the animal, and secondly to ask the man to put the dog on a leash. He did so silently, and I continued my patrol.

A few minutes later I was again greeted by the very happy dog racing up to the vehicle, and again I asked the owner to leash the dog. Again, he did so, all without a word.

By the third time, I was getting fed up.

"Mate," I told the owner, as he carefully looked at his shoes, "I could quite possibly run over your dog. One of our conditions of requirement to the bush here is that you keep your dog on a leash. Could you *please* leash your dog?"

That was the last time I came across them that day, but I did catch glimpses of them every now and then on later days, usually across the creek, running and off-leash.

The second type of unleashed-dog owner is the one who try to bluff their way out of leashing their dog. They argue that their dog is very well-behaved and would never cause any problems, all whilst the subject canine is bounding cheerfully through the undergrowth, trampling vegetation, and eroding the creek bank. Too often they feel encouraged by seeing others who also walk their dogs without leashes; after all, if *that* person's dog can be off a leash, why should their dog be leashed?

The third type of unleashed-dog walker is the aggressive ones. The ones who act like the bushland is their own backyard and they have every right to treat it as they like. Telling them the bushland is private property is like a personal insult. And when you are faced with an aggressive person with a dog, it is wiser to choose safety.

That sense of entitlement is a common theme that runs behind many of the human impacts that the bushland faces. The majority of the time, the bush was fairly clean, with only the occasional single-use plastic water bottle floating in the creek. But sometimes, in the less trafficked parts of the bush, we would stumble across the remains of someone's party - dozens of glass bottles that once held beer or vodka, empty energy drink cans, DIY drug paraphernalia, and the scattered remains of junk food packets. Once we found a tent filled with these things and carted it away; the owners were obviously not pleased with this turn of events as when we returned to check the site the following week, a small sapling had been manually uprooted and unceremoniously thrown down where the tent had been.

People can be selfish.

Like the time some of our bush regenerator discovered a hatchet-wielding passerby had chopped down a few of our younger trees, leaving the lopped upper halves lying beside the stumps of their bodies.

Like the time a few of us painstaking chopped through clay and dodged sandstone to plant some small native species to control erosion along a shortcut some walkers had created, and we came back the next day to find most of the plants had not only been torn out, but hurled a considerable distance off the track, or completely trampled into the ground.

It is easy to become angry.

So much time and effort, so much love of nature and dedication to our work, years of rain and slow growth, to be destroyed within minutes.

It is easy to feel frustrated and hopeless.

Stand for a moment, staring wordlessly at the damage and trying to process it. When that passes, slowly start to try and salvage something, anything, retrieving the plants that can be retrieved, cutting away damaged limbs, replanting, barricading, hoping that they will grow.

On the other hand, there are those people who embrace the bush whole-heartedly. Every now and then, a rudimentary humpy would appear by the banks of Coups Creek, tiny shelters made of sticks and palm fronds, most likely by the local kids. Fun as they are, the site is too small and delicate to allow us to encourage activities that require damaging vegetation, so we always remove them after admiring the handiwork.

Even now, humanity continues to produce new words relating to nature to explain the connections and losses we are experiencing. In 1964, two scientists from CSIRO created 'petrichor', the smell of soil as it absorbs moisture, particularly just before, during or just after a rain event. Siliceous materials are especially good at producing this smell, which is admittedly my favourite in the world and a distinctive one that many people find refreshing. In 1974, a scientist of the University of Minnesota coined 'topophilia' to encompass a love of place and the perceptions and values people hold towards those places.

On the other hand, in 2003, an Australian philosopher coined 'solastalgia', the feeling of grief experienced when the landscape one is living in changes for the worse, particularly due to environmental damage. He was thinking of the experiences of those living in the Hunter Valley near open cut mines, their sense of loss as their homes changed around them.

We are, all of us, humans and plants and animals, creatures of this world. There is no arguing otherwise, and so we keep going.

Above: Volunteers and bush workers alike enjoy a well-earned break. Below (L-R): A young volunteer helps plant a tree; A tour group admires the Sydney Blue Gums.

Above: Volunteers help gather seeds. Below: A proud group after a hard day's weeding.

Epilogue

Sometimes I could see it, the forest before the logging and the feral animals and white man. A dense tangle stretching up to tall Red Cedars, the constant calling of small birds and the soft *thump* of a wallaby. The ferns close in, secretively, only opening to the airier, lighter woodland on the higher reaches of the valley.

In those moments when the images sprang up in my mind, I would somnambulate along the trails until someone called out to me, and I remembered what I was seeing was not the present, in spite of how much it seemed I could reach out and touch it. After all, this was reality a little over a century ago – less than a heartbeat in the slow rhythms of the living world. Within the lifetime of a tree, these changes have taken place. It will take several more of their lifetimes to restore this forest.

And this is the truth, no matter where I go. In the months following my move north, away from the Wahroonga bush, I have seen the many ways humanity has changed the landscape. We continue to do the best we can, although it is not always easy to tell what is best.

I came back to Wahroonga for a day, to visit the bush team and see how the valley was progressing. Regeneration sites I had helped to plant were flourishing, new projects had been started, the work continued.

Sitting amongst the Golden Pittosporum (*Pittosporum revolutum*) in the understorey of the Sydney Turpentine Ironbark Forest, I pressed my bare hands to the earth and let the sense of wellbeing fill me. A magpie gargled melodiously in the *Yanderra* overhead.

My reverie was broken by the call of my old boss. "Pack up, everyone. It's coffee time!"

Laughing and chatting, we downed tools and made our way out of the bush.

EPILOGUE

Afterword

Revising this book in 2025 has been an interesting experience. Many things have changed since then, many things have happened. I have only had the opportunity to return to Coups Creek once, following the establishment of the dog park.

Which dog park, you ask? One of my last tasks before leaving was to apply for a grant to establish a fenced area for dogs to run about off-leash, given the tendency of many dog owners in the area to treat the whole conservation site as a dog park. I left before I saw the results of the grant, but later discovered it had been approved, built, and, somewhat embarrassingly, named after me.

The Frances O'Brien Dog Park is a modest size, with a picnic bench, under the trees in the east of the site. It resembles more a picnic area, and the Google Reviews have not been the most appreciative. At time of writing, there are two reviews, the first being a one-star review:

"Nothing but a dark and damp fenced area where dogs are permitted. Dog Area or Pen would describe it better"

and a two-star review:

"Secret forest fenced space between walking path & homes. Low fencing, two non-safe gates facing path & one privete gate at rear of a home."

For certain, this is a relatively small area, with fences more suited to keep in smaller dogs or perhaps children. It's the sort of place you might have a picnic… and one day I plan to do so with a collection of friends.

It's a strange experience, returning to a place you once knew so well. It's no longer *yours*, and the once familiar sights have changed. Seeing the dog park again, which I had only seen once before, in the company of friends, will likely be an odd but precious experience. Perhaps I will see the bowerbird too, foraging near his bower, or the Eastern Water Dragons in the creek nearby. I'll sit under the blue gums in the sun and look at the sign on the fence bearing my full name, which I rarely use these days.

So many things change. It is my fervent wish, however, that this little piece of bushland stays green for many years to come.

Photo Credits

- Powerful Owl preening – Jillian Nolan
- Sun shining through trees – Frankie O'Brien (page 1)
- Coups Creek with Bleeding Heart leaf – Jillian Nolan (page 14)
- Smoke in the trees – Frankie O'Brien (page 14)
- Foggy morning – Frankie O'Brien (page 15)
- Sandstone cliffs – Consuelo Gonzalez (page 15)
- Satin Bowerbird – Jillian Nolan (page 17)
- Peron's Tree Frog – Frankie O'Brien (page 40)
- *Aenetus scotti* – Frankie O'Brien (page 40)
- King Parrot preening – Jillian Nolan (page 40)
- Diamond Python – Jillian Nolan (page 41)
- Tawny Frogmouth – Wahroonga Waterways Landcare (page 41)
- Ringtail Possum – Jillian Nolan (page 41)
- Spotted Sun Orchid – Wahroonga Waterways Landcare (page 43)
- Fungi – Frankie O'Brien (page 55)
- *Dianella caerulea* flowers – Wahroonga Waterways Landcare (page 55)
- Wombat Berry – Wahroonga Waterways Landcare (page 56)
- Dainty Bird Orchid – Frankie O'Brien (page 56)
- Bush regen team with the tree – Frankie O'Brien (page 57)
- Morning tea – Consuelo Gonzalez (page 73)
- Young volunteer - Wahroonga Waterways Landcare (page 73)
- Blue Gum with tour group – Jillian Nolan (page 73)
- Volunteer seed gathering – Jillian Nolan (page 74)
- Weeding team – Elissa Avery (page 74)
- Frances O'Brien Dog Park – Elissa Avery (page 79)

PHOTO CREDITS

www.ingramcontent.com/pod-product-compliance
Lightning Source LLC
Chambersburg PA
CBHW070434290526
45791CB00005B/1965